Clean and Healthy

Angela Royston

Heinemann Library
Des Plaines, Illinois

Text designed by Celia Floyd
Printed and bound in Hong Kong, China

04 03 02 01 00
10 9 8 7 6 5 4 3 2 1

Library of Congress Cataloging-in-Publication Data
Royston, Angela.
    Clean and healthy / Angela Royston.
        p. cm. – (Safe and sound)
    Includes bibliographical references and index.
    Summary: Explores basic concepts of healthy living, including cleanliness, safety, and regular medical care.
    ISBN 1-57572-981-4
    1. Health Juvenile literature. 2. Diseases Juvenile literature.
    3. Children—Health and hygiene Juvenile literature. [1. Health.]
    I. Title. II. Series: Royston, Angela. Safe and sound.
    R130.5.R688 1999
    C13—dc21   99-14555
                                                              CIP

Acknowledgments
The author and publishers are grateful to the following for permission to reproduce photographs:
Bubbles/Dr. H. Robinson, pp. 28, 29; F. Rombout, p. 27; J. Allan Cash, Ltd., p. 16; Trevor Clifford, pp. 5, 7, 8, 9, 10, 11, 12, 13, 14, 15, 18, 19, 20, 22, 23; Format/M. Murray, p. 17; Carol Palmer, p. 25; Science Photo Library/M. Clarke, pp. 21, 26; Dr. L. Stannard, UCT, p. 6; H. Young, p. 24; Tony Stone Images/P. Cade, p. 4.

Cover photo: Trevor Clifford

Every effort has been made to contact copyright holders of any material reproduced in this book. Any omissions will be rectified in subsequent printings if notice is given to the publisher.

The Publishers would like to thank Julie Johnson, PSHE consultant and trainer, for her comments in the preparation of this book.

Some words in this book are in bold, **like this.** You can find out what they mean by looking in the glossary.

Contents

Soap and Water

When you play outside, you may get muddy and dirty. As soon as you come in you should wash away the dirt, especially from your hands and face.

Keeping clean protects you from **germs** that can make you unhealthy. In this book you will learn lots of ways to keep clean and healthy.

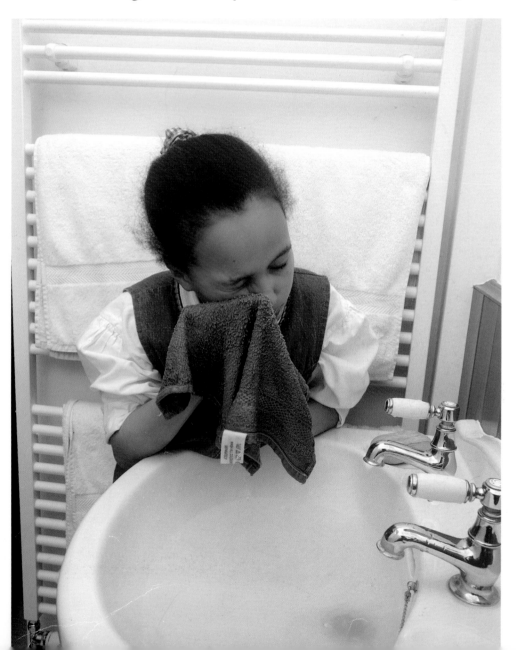

What Are Germs?

Germs are tiny living things. Germs are thousands of times smaller than this—too small to see without a **microscope**. This is how germs look under a microscope.

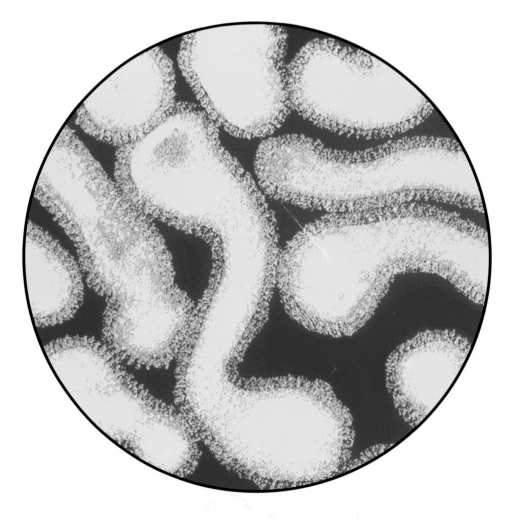

Some germs can make you sick if they get inside your body. They can cause **diseases**. Sneezing is one way your body gets rid of germs.

How Germs Spread

Germs can pass from one person to another. When you have a cold, germs leave your body each time you sneeze, cough, or breathe out.

Other people may breathe in some of your germs. Make sure you cover your mouth when you cough. This will stop the germs from spreading through the air.

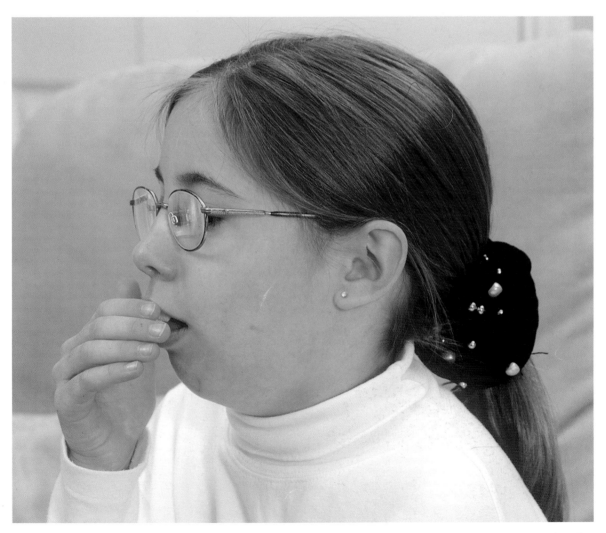

Wash Your Hands!

Washing your hands helps keep **germs** from spreading. It is especially important to wash your hands well with soap and water after going to the toilet.

It is very easy for germs to spread from your hands into your mouth. Always wash your hands before you eat any food.

Clean Food

You may take in **germs** when you eat, drink, or put something in your mouth. If food falls on the ground or gets dirty, throw it away.

There are germs everywhere, so be careful what you put in your mouth. Pens and pencils, even your thumb, may be covered with germs.

Pets

Pets are fun to play with. Cats, dogs, and many other pets love to be petted. But their fur and mouths may be full of **germs**.

Don't let your pet lick your face or mouth. Wash your hands well with soap and water after you play with your pet.

Wild Animals

It is fun to feed ducks and other **birds**. Remember, many wild animals have **fleas**. Their **droppings** carry **germs**.

Some wild animals spread dangerous germs. Don't play near areas where there could be rats or other **pests**.

Don't Touch Blood

Blood can carry dangerous **germs**. Never touch anyone else's blood. If your friend has a cut, give him or her some clean paper to put over it.

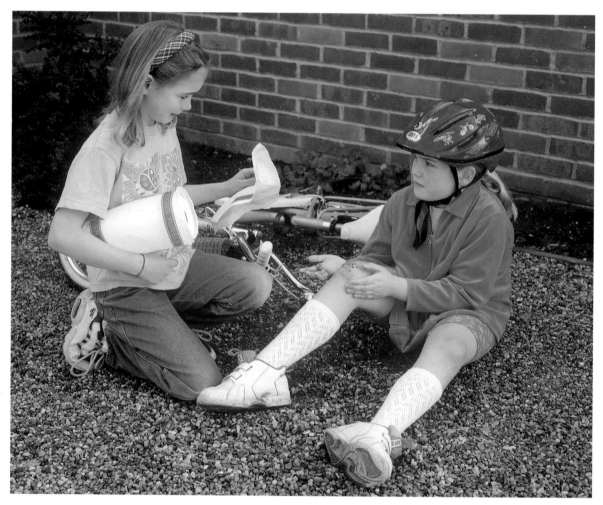

Always ask a grown-up to clean a cut. Put a bandage on to protect the **wound** and keep it clean while it heals.

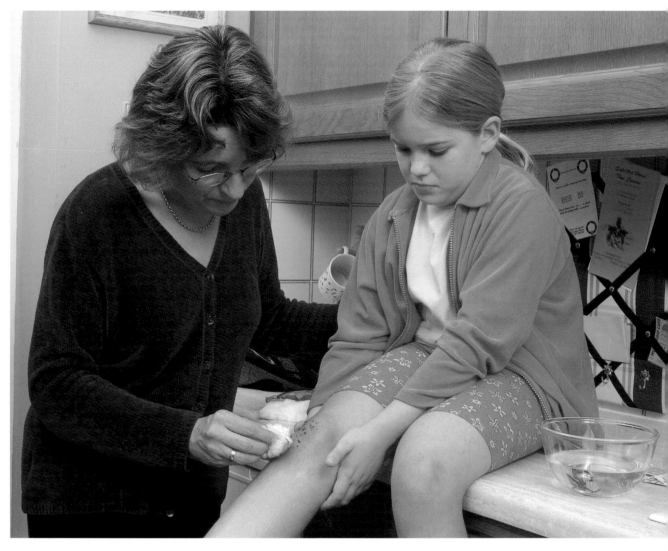

Hair Care

Head lice are tiny insects that can live in your hair. They make your head itch. They can spread quickly from one person to another. You can catch them by using someone else's comb or hat.

Keep your hair and clothes clean. You can comb your hair with a special comb. Check to see if there are any head lice on it. If there are, you may need to use a special shampoo to get rid of them.

Brush Your Teeth!

You should brush your teeth at least twice a day. Food left in your mouth turns into **germs** that make **acid**. Acid can make holes in your teeth.

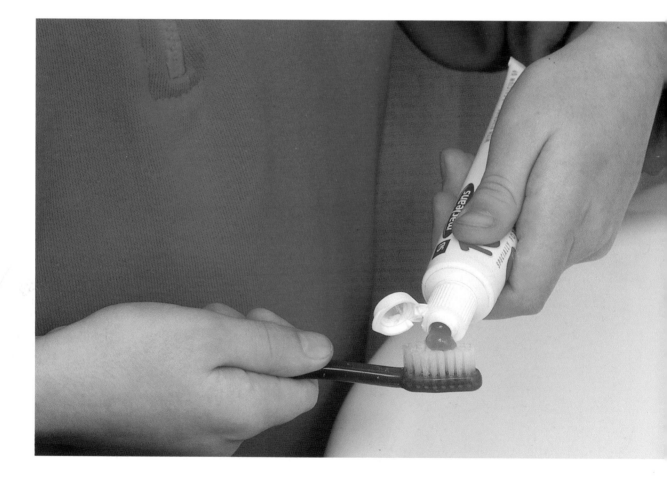

Make sure you brush the front and back of your teeth from the gums to the tips. Then brush the tops of the big teeth at the back of your mouth.

Visiting the Dentist

You should visit the dentist every six months. The dentist will check to see if all of your teeth are strong and healthy.

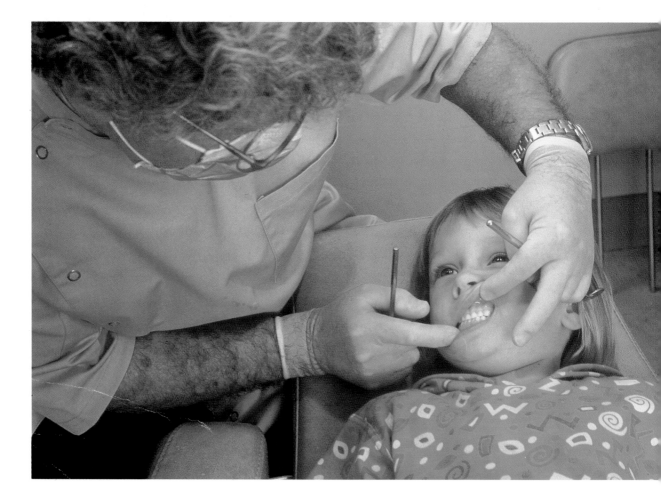

Your teeth will be cleaned and polished with a special brush. The dentist may show you how to use **dental floss** to keep your teeth clean.

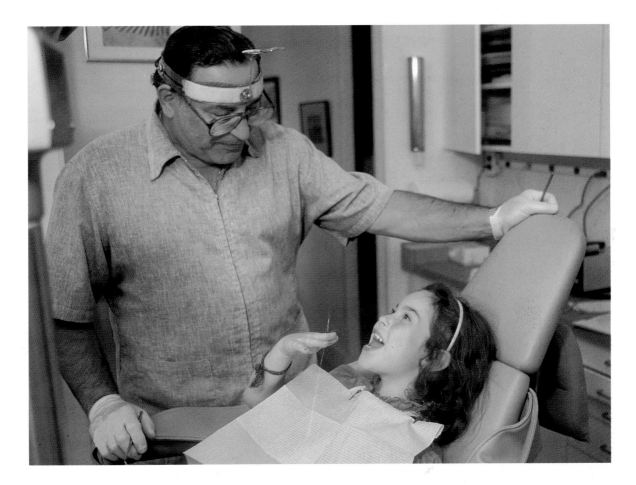

Visiting the Doctor

You should have a checkup once a year. The doctor will check your whole body to make sure you are healthy.

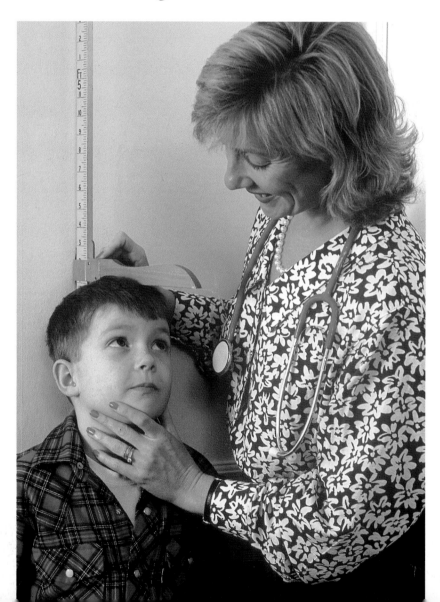

A doctor or nurse will check to see how much you weigh and how tall you are. He or she may also check how well you see and hear.

Keeping Well

Even though you feel healthy, you may need a
vaccination. A **vaccine** helps your body fight and
kill a serious **disease** before it can make you sick.

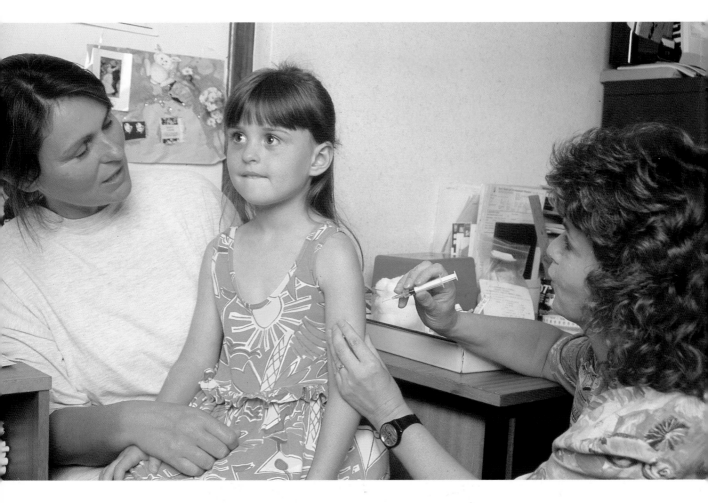

Many vaccines are **injected**. Some are dropped straight into your mouth. Vaccinations are an important part of staying healthy and strong.

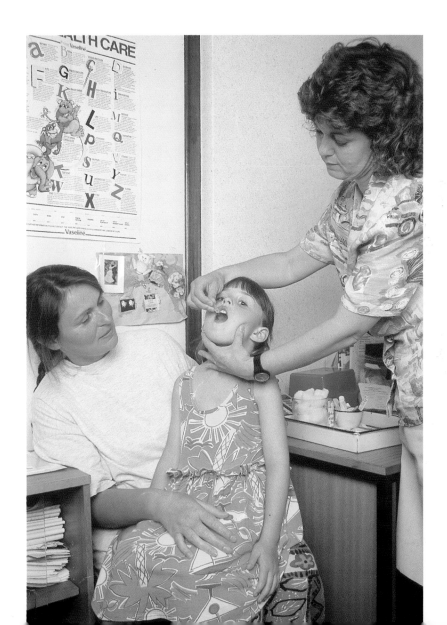

Glossary

acid   sour-tasting liquid that can make holes in your teeth

blood   red liquid that carries food and oxygen around the body

dental floss   type of thread used to clean between the teeth

disease   sickness

dropping   animal waste

flea   tiny insect that lives on an animal's body

germ   tiny living thing that can get inside the body and make you sick

head louse   (more than one are called **lice**) insect that lives in the hair and lays eggs on the hair close to the head

inject to push a liquid into the body with a needle

microscope instrument that uses lenses to make things look larger than they really are

pest living thing that can cause damage or disease

vaccination when weak germs are put into the body to help fight off a disease—also sometimes called a shot

vaccine small dose of dead or weak germs that the body can easily kill. The body is then always ready to kill germs before they can make you sick.

wound injury, like a cut or a bruise, not caused by a sickness

Index

More Books to Read

Boelts, Maribeth, and Darwin Boelts. *Kids to the Rescue! First-Aid Techniques for Kids.* Seattle: Parenting Press, 1992.

Greenberg, Keith E. *Disease Detective.* Woodbridge, Conn.: Blackbirch Press, 1998. An older reader can help you with this book.

Hundley, David H. *Bruises.* Vero Beach, Fla.: Rourke Press, 1998.